LOST TREASURE MAZES

Roger Moreau

Sterling Publishing Co., Inc.
New York

10   9   8   7   6   5   4   3   2   1

Published by Sterling Publishing Company, Inc.
387 Park Avenue South, New York, N.Y. 10016
© 1999 by Roger Moreau
Distributed in Canada by Sterling Publishing
C/o Canadian Manda Group, One Atlantic Avenue, Suite 105
Toronto, Ontario, Canada M6K 3E7
Distributed in Great Britain and Europe by Chris Lloyd
463 Ashley Road, Parkstone, Poole, Dorset, BH14 0AX, England
Distributed in Australia by Capricorn Link (Australia) Pty Ltd.
P.O. Box 6651, Baulkham Hills, Business Centre, NSW 2153, Australia
Manufactured in the United States of America

Sterling ISBN 0-8069-7811-2

CONTENTS

A Note on the Suggested Use of This Book   4

Introduction   5

S.S. *Central America*   6

The Treasure Map   8

The *Concepcion's* Treasure   10

The Treasure of Pinaki Atoll   12

The Money Pit 1   14

The Money Pit 2   15

The Lost Dutchman Mine   16

Return to Phoenix   18

Victorio Peak   20

Sutro's Tunnel   22

Genoa's Buried Treasure   24

The Trail to King John's Castle   25

The Courtyard   26

The Banquet Room   28

King John's Throne Room   30

The Trek   32

Canyon Land   34

The Ruins   36

The Lost Mayan temple   37

Oh No, Snakes   38

The Gold Idol   40

Congratulations   42

Treasure Guides   43

Index   64

A NOTE ON THE SUGGESTED USE OF THIS BOOK

Don't use a marker on the mazes in this book. Use a pointer instead so that you do not reveal your work. Then you can reuse the book at a future date or see if one of your friends can be as successful as your are.

Cover maze: It looks as if a great fight is about to take place. Should you wait? No! Treasure has too great a lure. Find your way around all of the sea life and swim down to the sunken treasure below.

INTRODUCTION

The two stagecoach robbers hid patiently just around one of the many sharp curves on the Kingbury grade just east of Lake Tahoe. Any minute now the stage, carrying $20,000 in gold for the Comstock payroll at Virginia City, would be slowing to make the turn. It was the perfect location for stopping the stage and performing their evil deed—stealing the treasure.

After a successful holdup, the robbers thought it would be wise to bury the gold at the base of a large pine tree near the town of Genoa at the end of the Kingbury grade and make their getaway. When the heat was off, they could return for the gold. Unplanned events occurred and they never returned. The treasure has never been found.

This story of lost treasure is not uncommon. Great treasures have been lost throughout history. The loss almost always occurs as a result of unplanned events—from natural disaster to murder—and is usually surrounded by rumor, mystery, and intrigue.

Many treasures lost in the inaccessible depths of the seas have been found and recovered thanks to modern detecting and submersible equipment. On land, metal detectors and sophisticated sonar equipment can help, but the main effort still requires backbreaking hours of research and legwork and often involves great danger. Even when the location of a treasure is known, the conditions for retrieving it are often highly unsafe and the danger is great. Nevertheless, the desire for wealth and the lure of the find can be so great that a few will take the risk and fewer still will occasionally have success. Some become so addicted to the quest that they spend a lifetime searching in vain for that elusive "lost treasure."

Now you have an opportunity to go forth in search of some of the greatest treasures ever lost. As with every hunt for lost treasure, there will be great danger. Don't give up. Your reward, if you are successful, will be beyond your wildest dreams.

S.S. Central America

In 1857, the side-wheeler S.S. *Central America* sank off the coast of Carolina in a

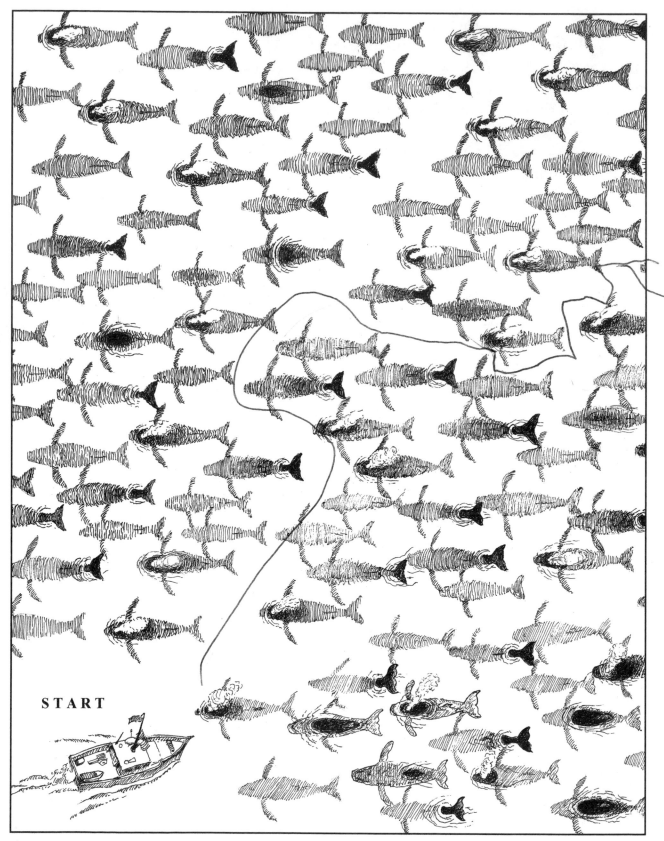

START

terrible hurricane with perhaps a billion dollars in gold on board. In 1985, this treasure was found and recovered. See if you have the skills to find the *Central America.* Stay clear of the migrating herd of whales and find your way to the ship.

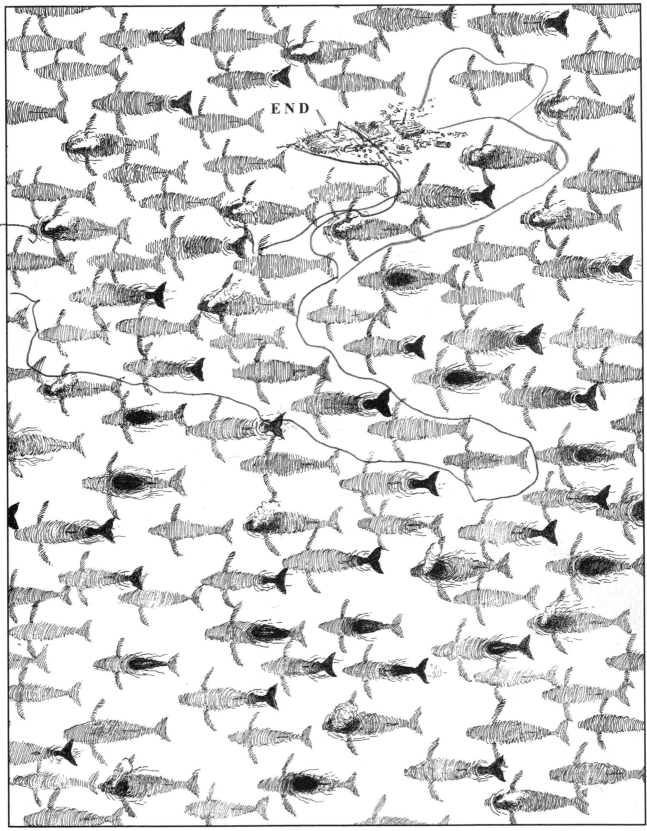

The Treasure Map

In 1641, the Spanish galleon *Concepcion*, already crippled by a hurricane, struck

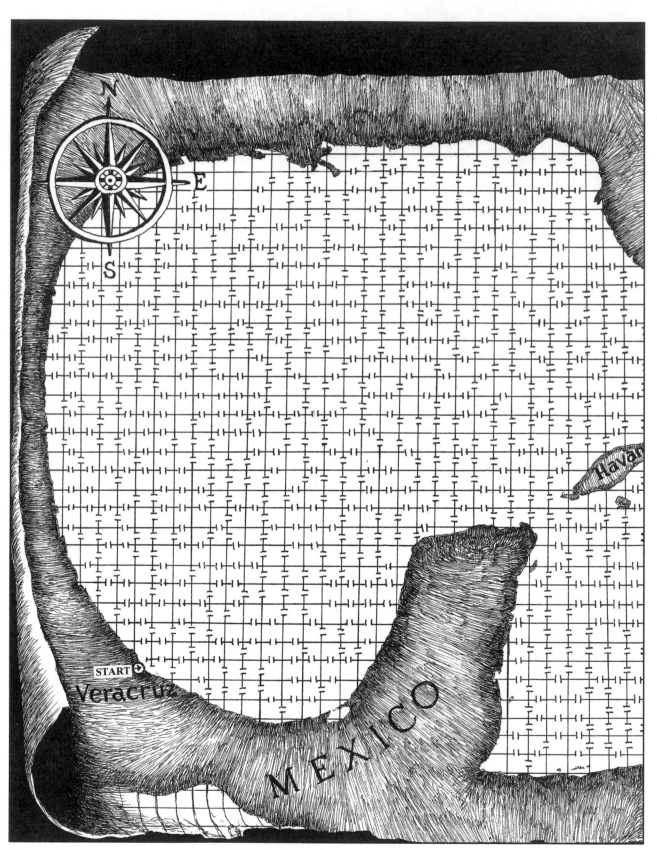

the treacherous Abrojos reef northeast of Hispaniola and sank with an exceptionally large treasure. Can you find where she went down? Use this map and sail through the openings to find a passage to the sunken ship.

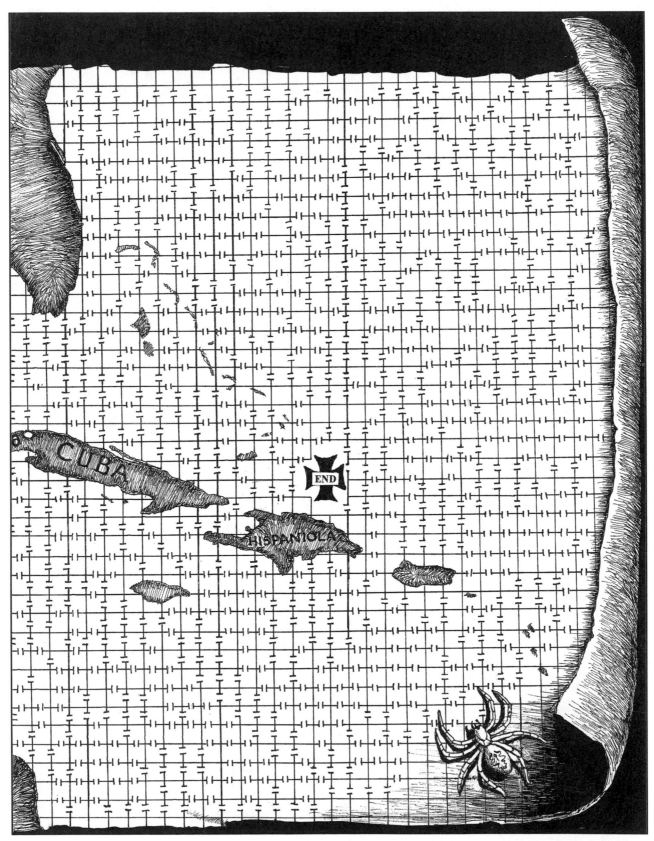

The *Concepcion's* Treasure

You have found the *Concepcion* and you know from the ship's logs from hundreds

START

of years ago that there is great treasure, Spanish *reales* and silver bars, to be recovered. However, in order to salvage the treasure you must avoid the dangerous sea life of the reef and find a clear route to the remains of the ship.

The Treasure of Pinaki Atoll

In the early 1880's, four Australian mercenaries buried a great treasure stolen

START

from Peru on Pinaki atoll. To this day it is still missing, and some believe it was located and dumped at sea to avoid a curse. Can you find a clear path to the treasure without disturbing the local sea life and then escape?

The Money Pit 1

This treasure was buried at the bottom of a deep sand pit. As you dig your way to the treasure, retrieve the coins as you go. You can go down and cross over into another pit, but you can not go up. Total your coins when you get to the bottom.

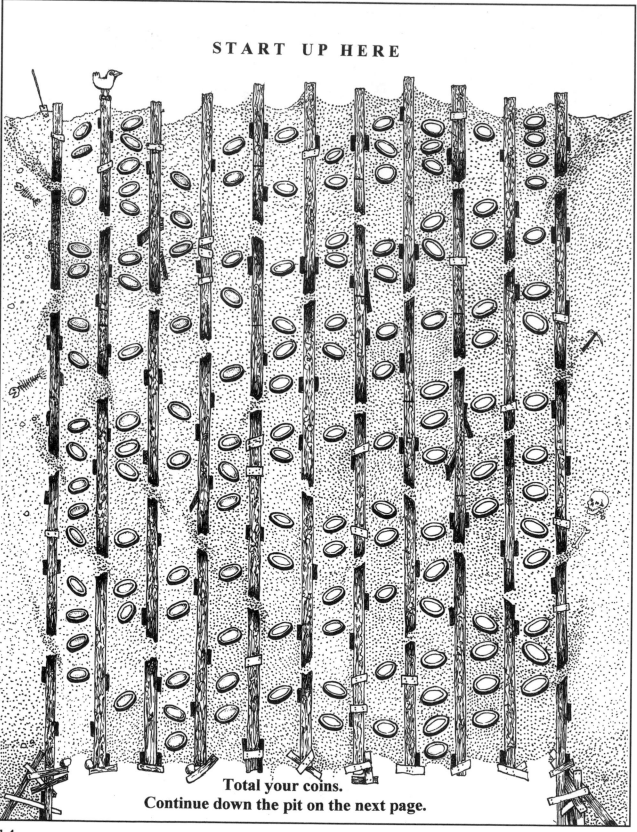

START UP HERE

Total your coins.
Continue down the pit on the next page.

The Money Pit 2

Continue down the pit starting at the top according to the number of coins you collected in pit 1. The same rules apply as in pit 1. You must have exactly 35 coins in order to obtain the key to open the treasure chests. Good luck.

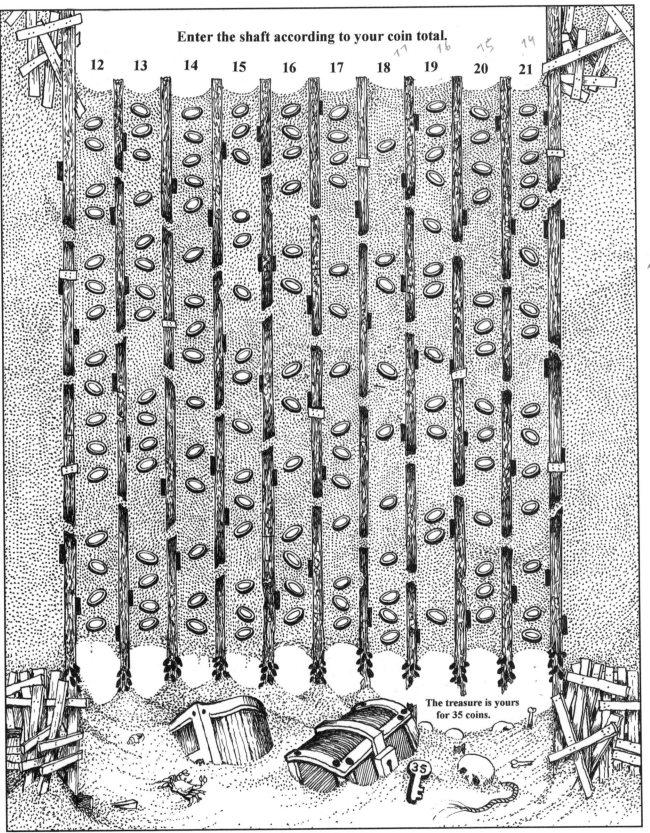

Enter the shaft according to your coin total.

12 13 14 15 16 17 18 19 20 21

The treasure is yours for 35 coins.

The Lost Dutchman Mine

The Lost Dutchman Mine is situated in the Superstition Mountains, 40 miles from

Phoenix, Arizona. Over the last century, many have travelled through sacred Indian land, into the mountains to find the mine and have never come out. Can you find a clear trail to the mine? Be careful. This is a dangerous quest.

Return to Phoenix

Now that you've found the mine, can you descend the mountain and get back to

Phoenix? The way back never looks the same as the way in—especially in the Superstition Mountains. You had better be very careful. There is danger at every turn.

Victorio Peak

The treasure of Emperor Maximilian of Mexico, thousands of bars of gold stacked

like cordwood along with 27 human skeletons, was found in a cave on Victorio Peak in New Mexico. When the entrance caved in, the treasure was lost. Find your way to Maximilian's gold by finding a clear passageway.

Sutro's Tunnel

The mines beneath Virginia City have filled with water. A lot of silver can still be

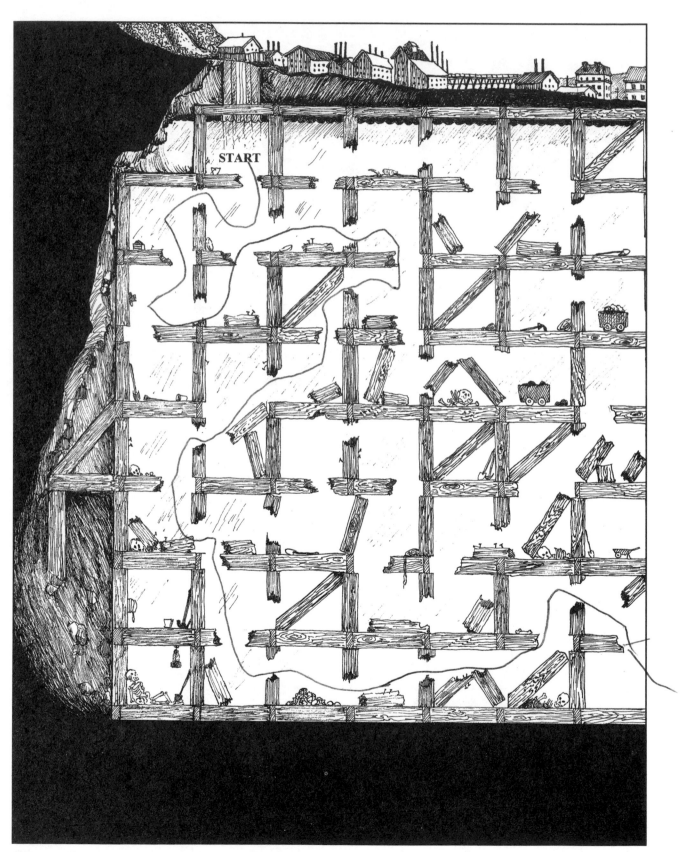

mined if the water can be drained. From 1869 to 1878, Adolph Sutro's crew dug a tunnel 4 miles under Virginia City to drain the mines, but now it is plugged. Swim down and blast away the plug.

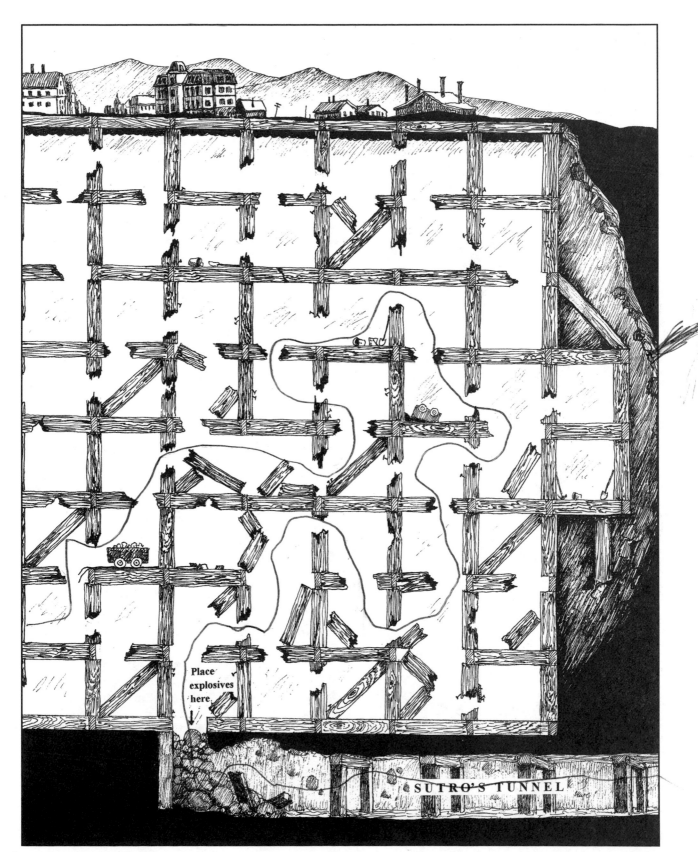

Place explosives here.

SUTRO'S TUNNEL

Genoa's Buried Treasure

An avalanche covered the gold buried at the foot of a pine near Genoa, Nevada. Check the tree bases. Do not backtrack, and visit each tree only once.

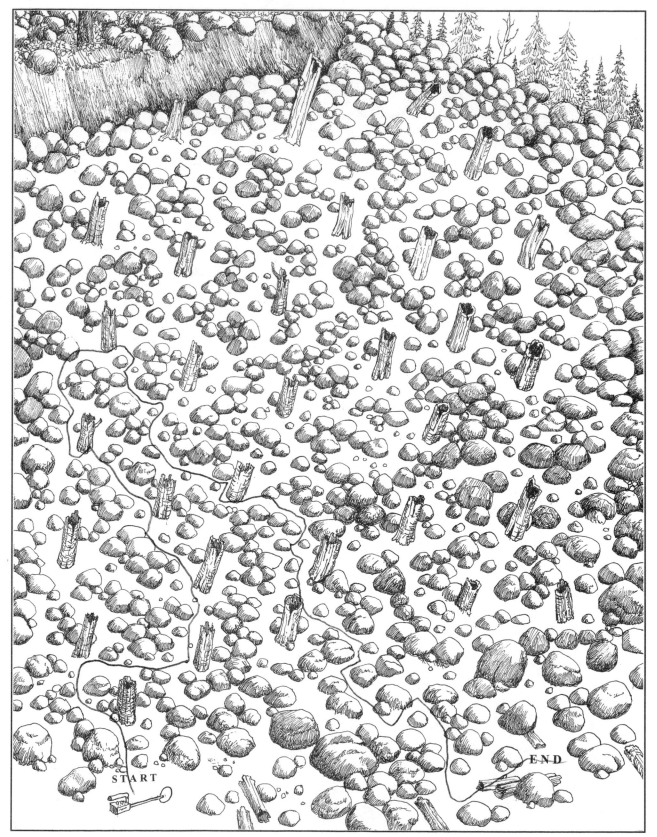

The Trail to King John's Castle

You are going to try and find the lost crown jewels of King John of England. Start down this trail on your way to his castle. Find a clear path.

The Courtyard

Cross through the courtyard to the castle. Enter at any one of the doors on the far side.

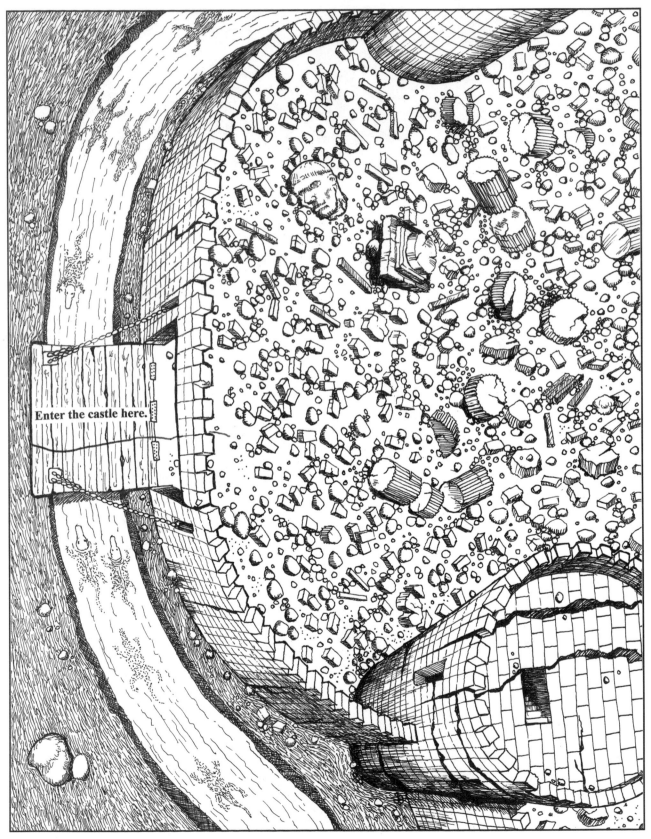

Enter the castle here.

Continue through one of these doors.

The Banquet Room

Cross through the banquet room without disturbing anything. Move into the next room through one of the three doors.

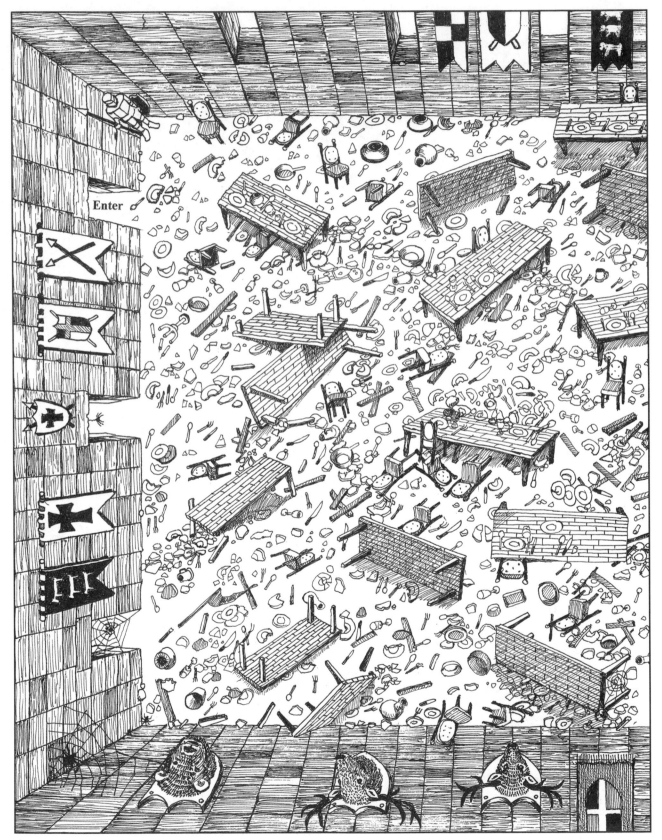

Enter

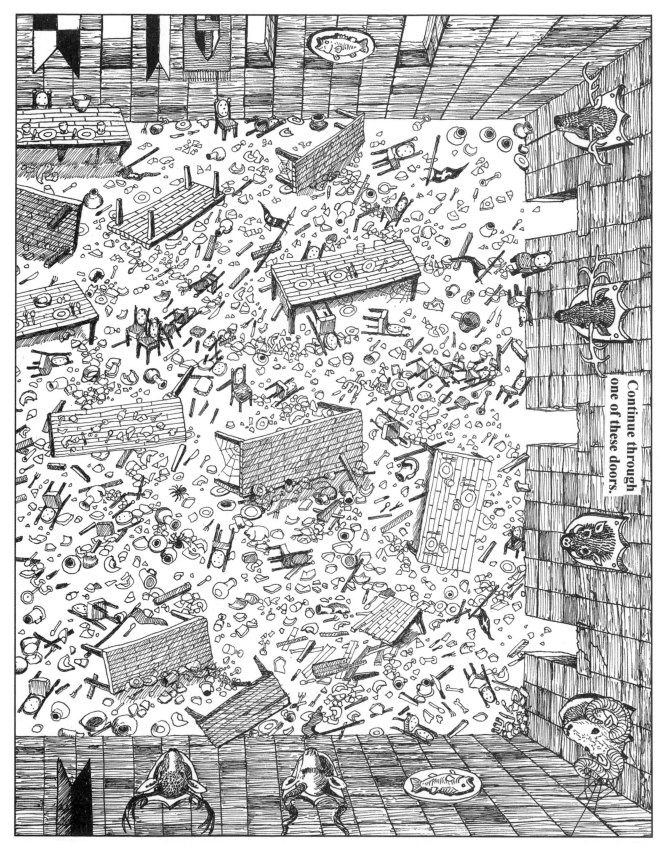

Continue through one of these doors.

29

King John's Throne Room

Many treasure robbers have tried to get to the treasure, which is guarded by brave knights. They have failed. Can you succeed? Find a clear path.

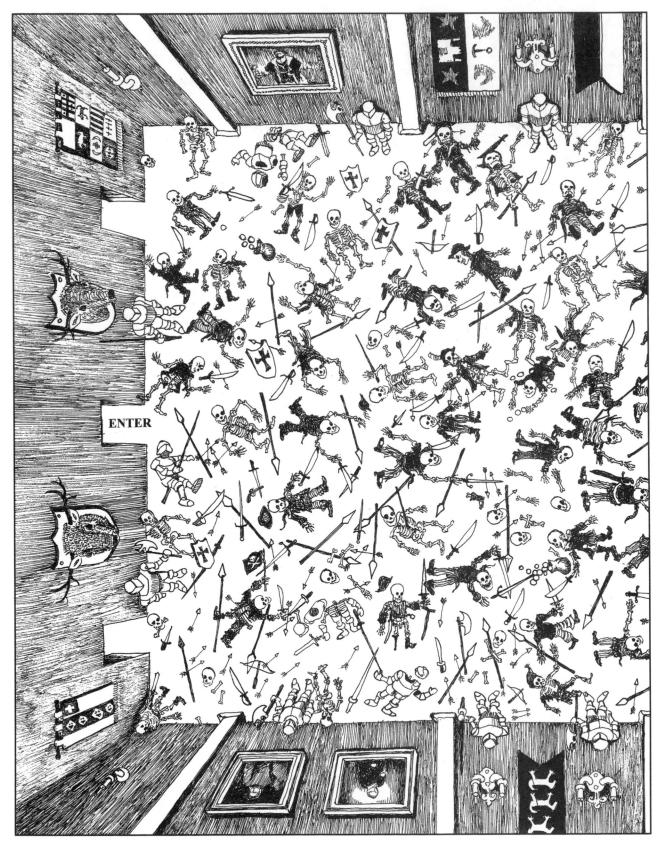

END

The Trek

Out there, somewhere in the jungles of Central America, is a lost Mayan Temple.

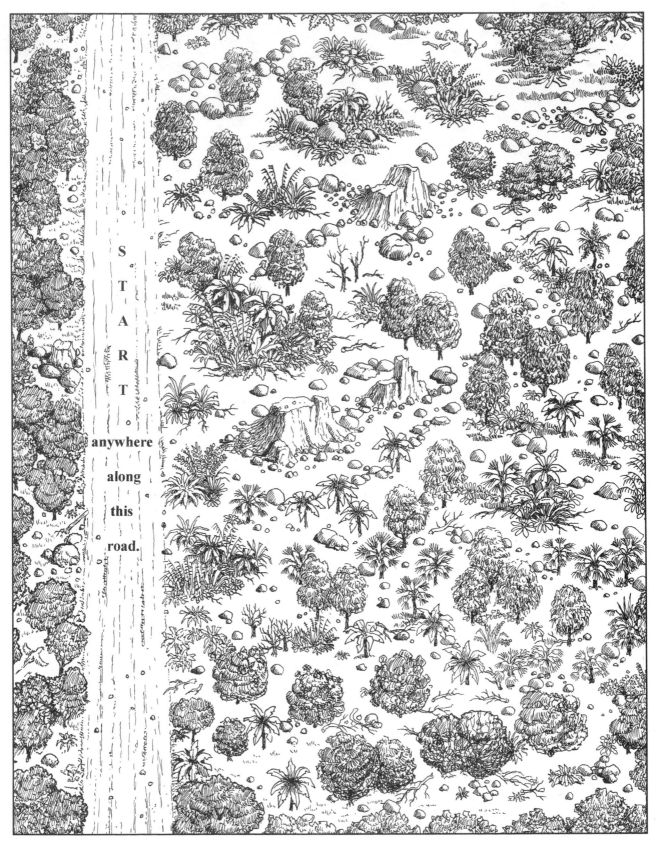

A search can be dangerous and take many days. Begin your trek to the right of the dirt road. You must find a clear path going east.

continue this way

Canyon Land

Continue east across the treacherous canyon land until you reach the gateway to the ruins.

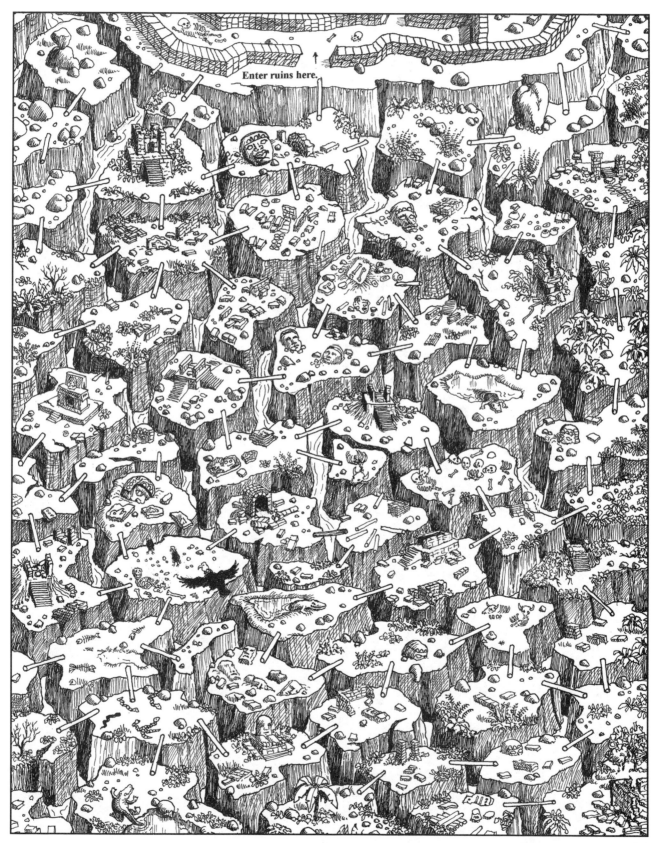

Enter ruins here.

The Ruins

Find your way through these ancient ruins to the temple steps ahead.

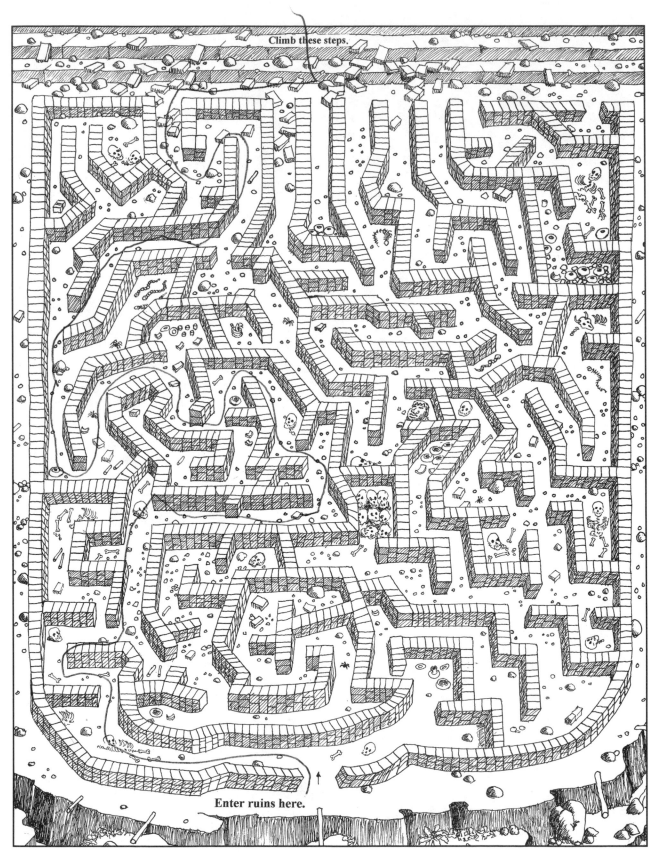

Climb these steps.

Enter ruins here.

The Lost Mayan Temple

You must pick your way across the ruins to reach the steps of the temple before you. Find a clear path.

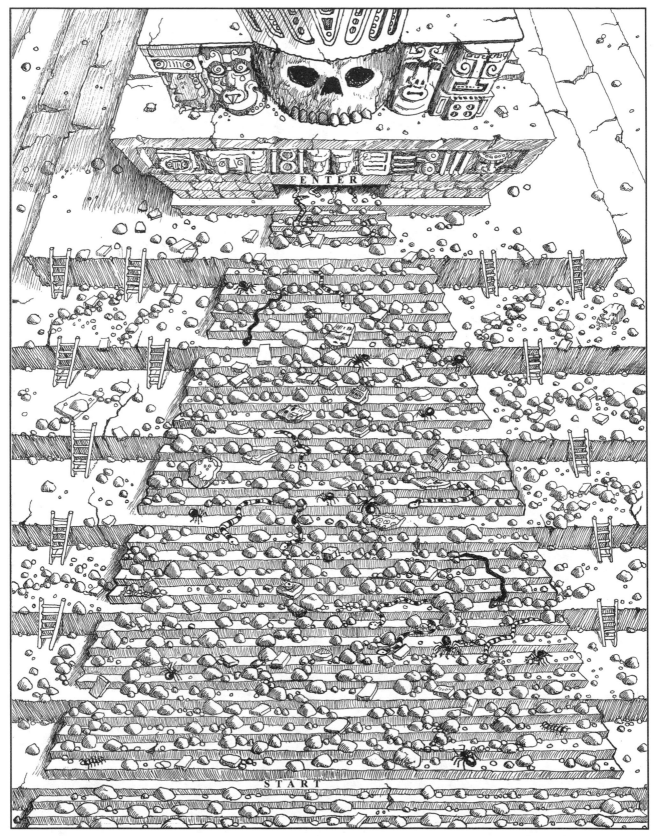

Oh No, Snakes

You must stay clear of all the snakes to reach the door at the top of the temple stairs.

THIS WAY...

The Gold Idol

This looks easy. Up ahead there seems to be a gold idol for the taking. But wait!

Notice that every dark tile is a trap door. Do not step on a dark tile and do not move at an angle—right and left turns only. If you reach the idol, you still must find your way out through one of the 13 remaining doors.

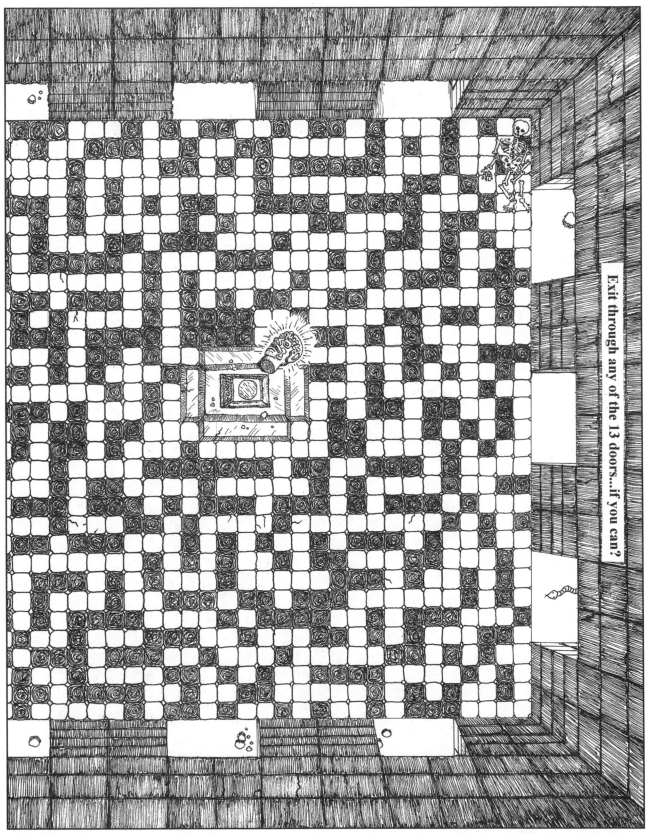

Exit through any of the 13 doors...if you can?

CONGRATULATIONS

Finding lost treasure has never been easy, as you now know. The keys to your success in these quests have been your courage, perseverance and dogged determination. Your rewards for these character traits have been great.

With the vast wealth that you now possess, your new challenge will be how to use it wisely. You will discover that using it for your own needs and self-indulgence will not bring you happiness or fulfillment. Certainly, you deserve some comforts, but only as you help others, in a world where great suffering occurs, will you experience real lasting joy.

May the world be a better place as a product of your thoughtfulness.

TREASURE GUIDE

If you had any trouble finding your way through the mazes in this book, use the treasure guide on the following pages. Do not use the guide to gain a treasure unfairly.

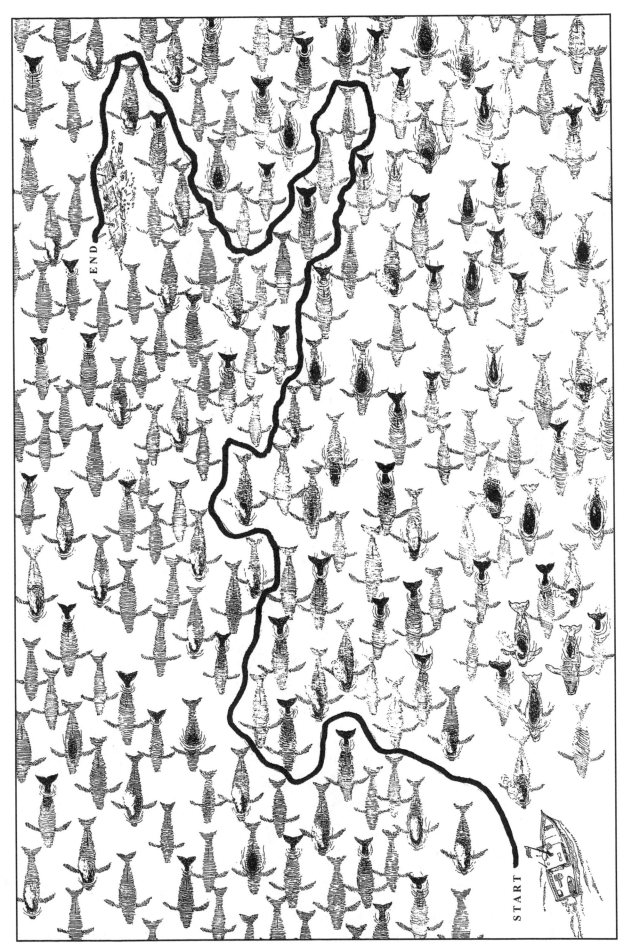

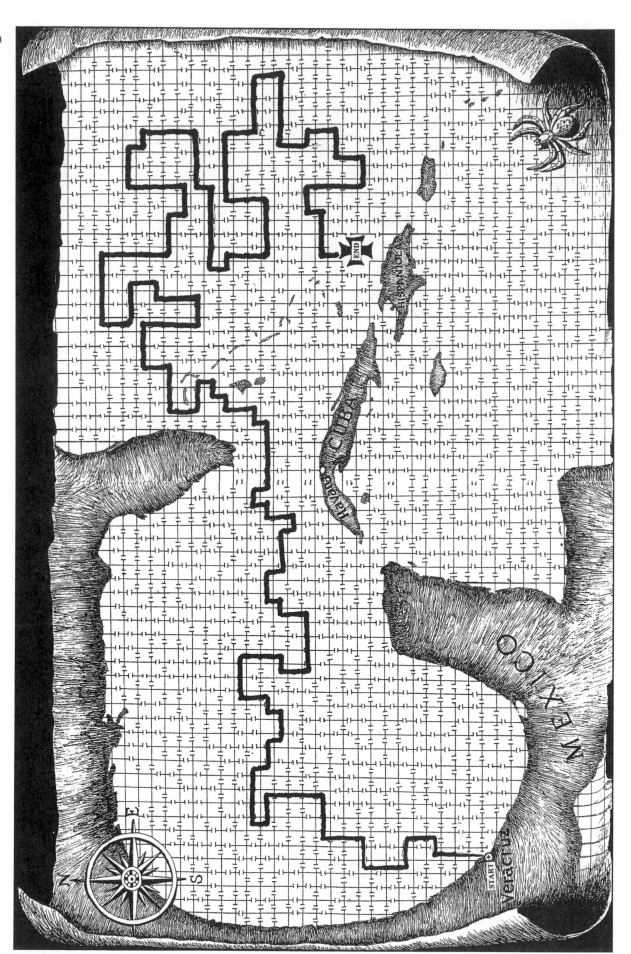

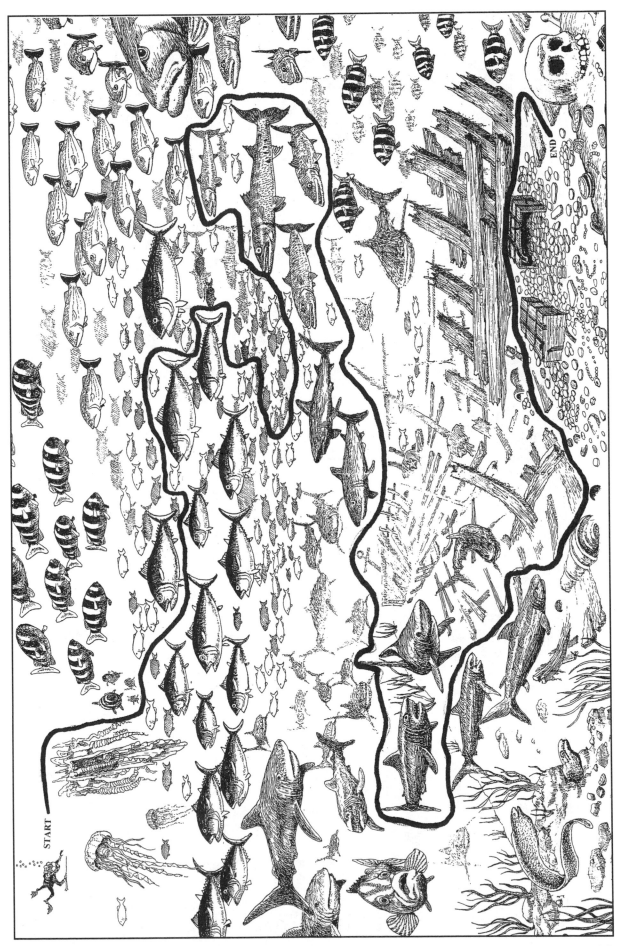

The *Concepcion's* Treasure

START

END

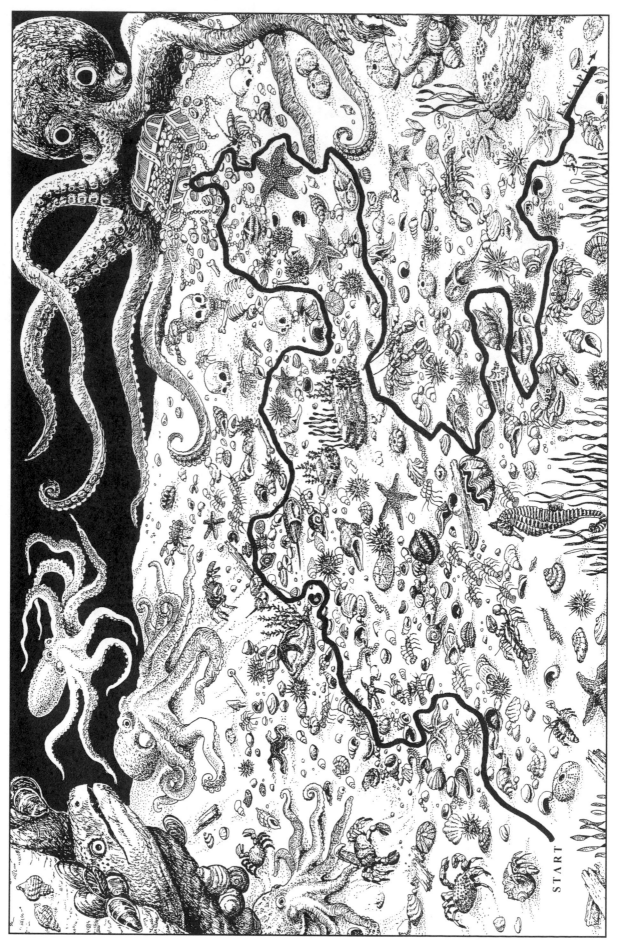

START

ESCAPE

STABT UP HERE

Total your coins.
Continue down the pit on the next page.

The Money Pit 2

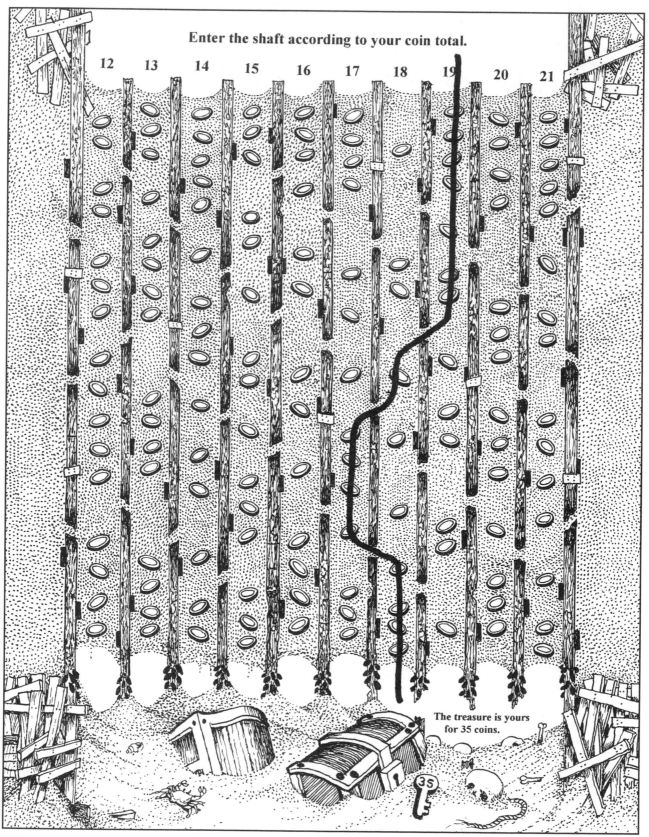

Enter the shaft according to your coin total.

12 13 14 15 16 17 18 19 20 21

The treasure is yours for 35 coins.

35

48

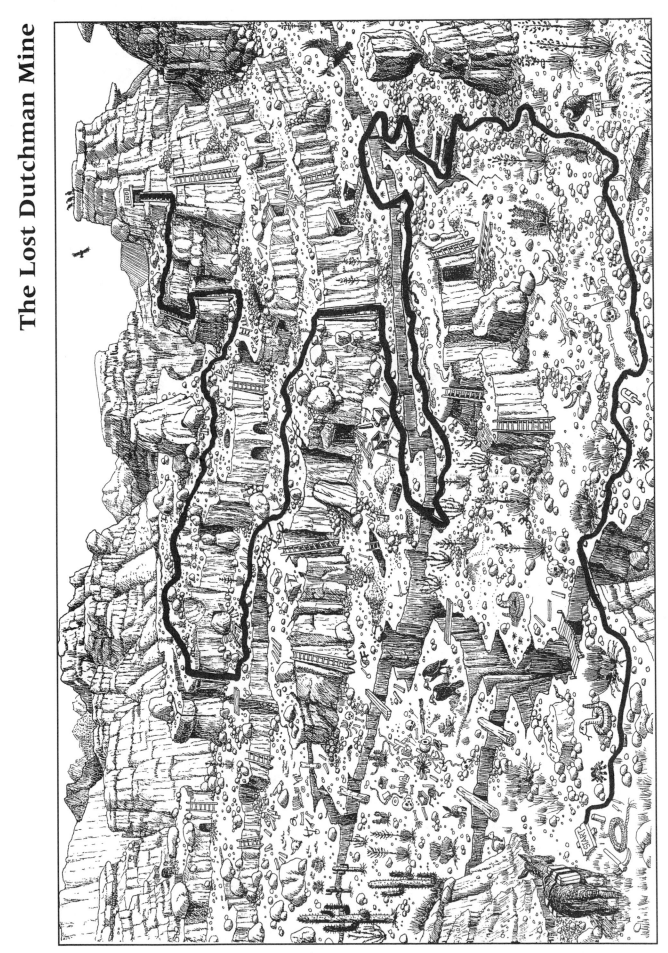

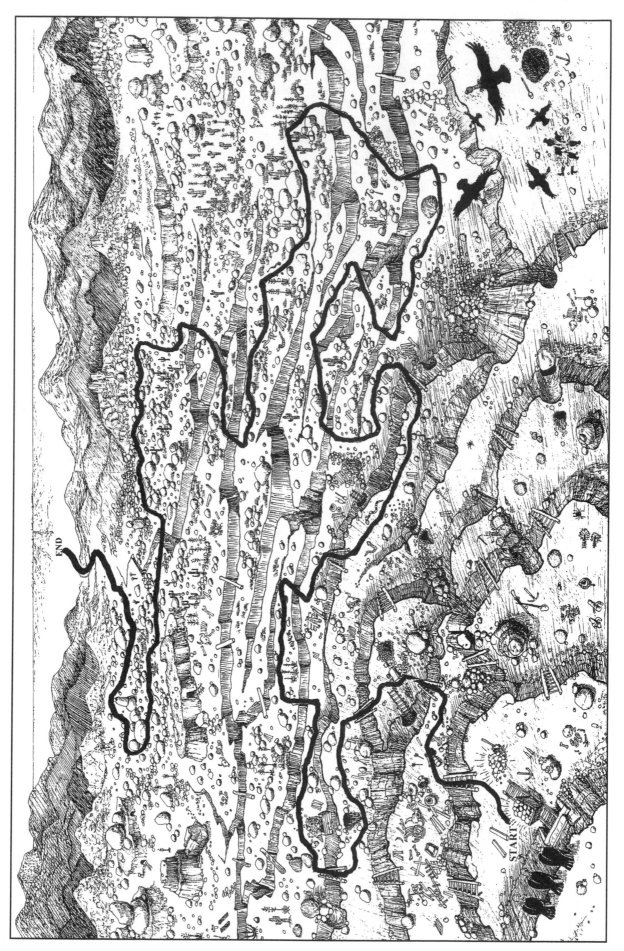

Victorio Peak

START

END DOWN HERE

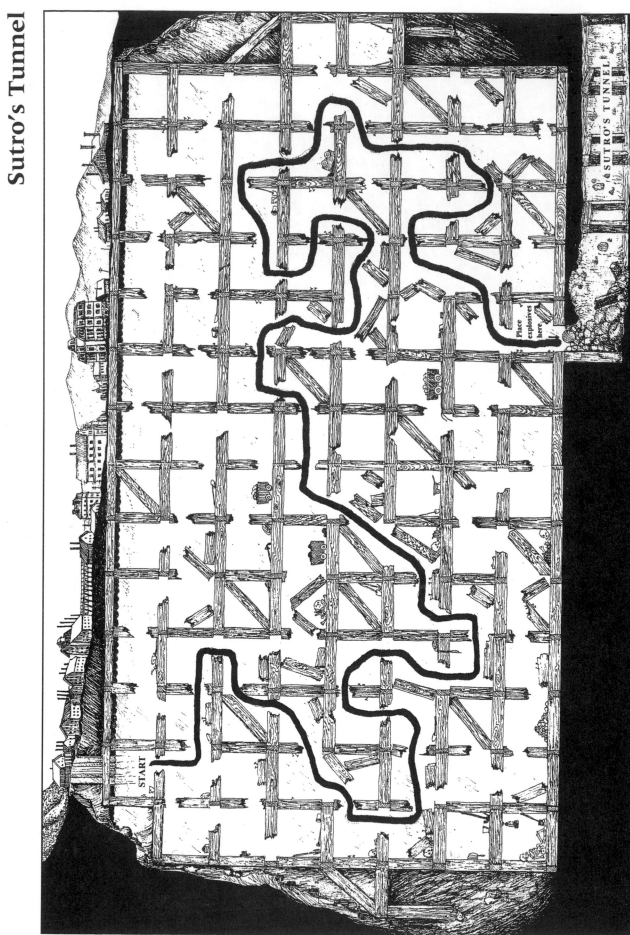

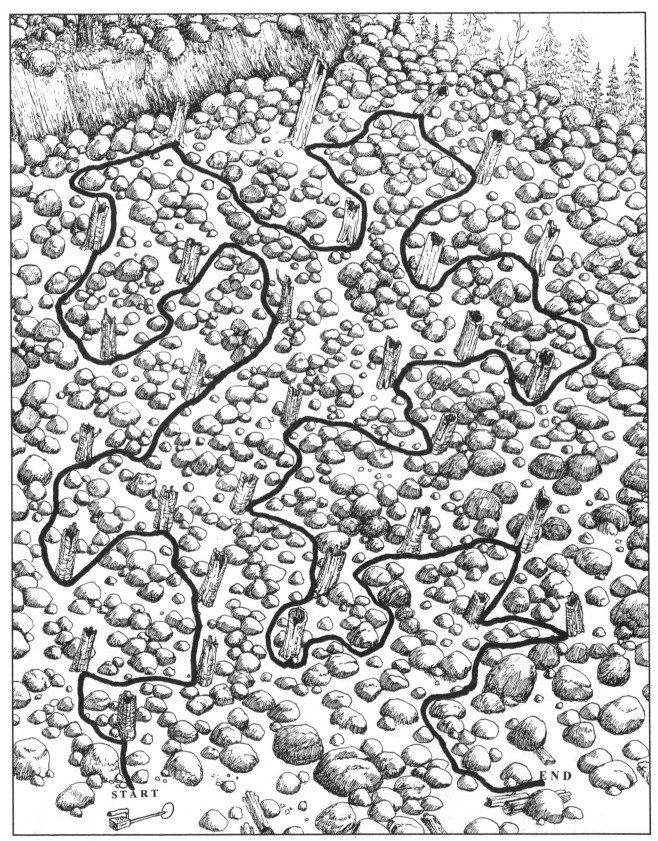

START

END

The Trail to King John's Castle

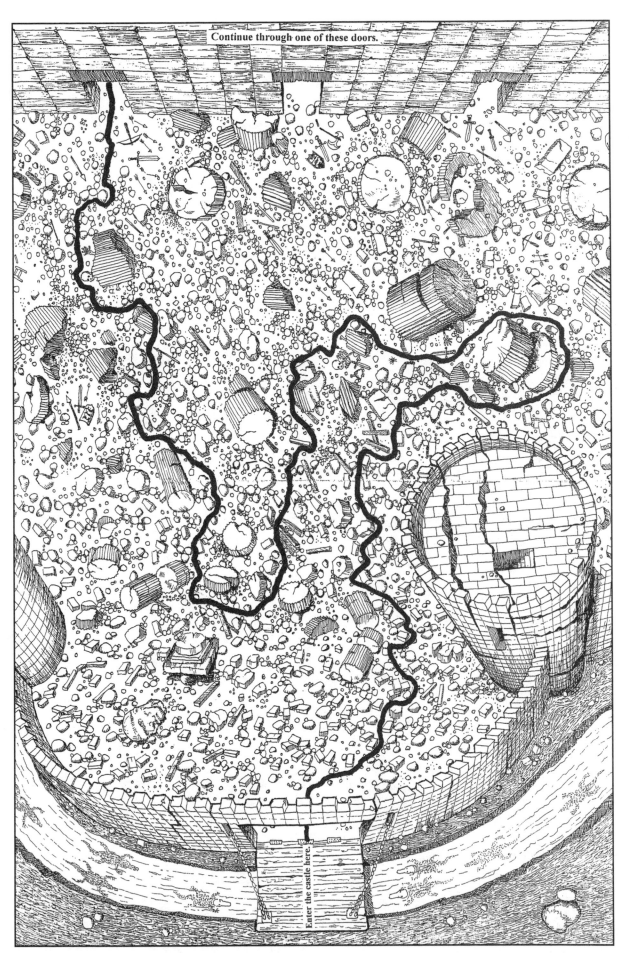

Continue through one of these doors.

Enter the castle here.

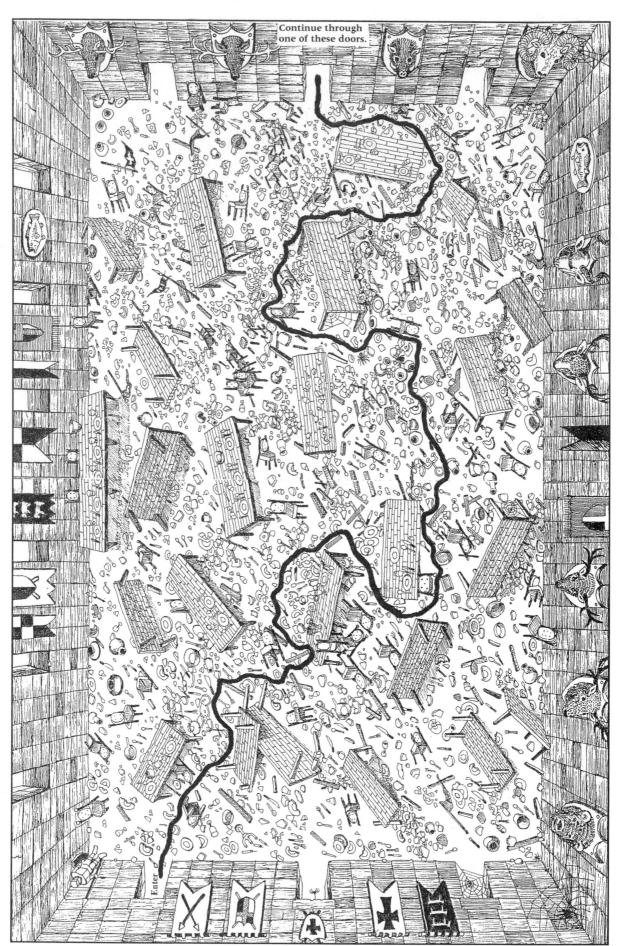

Continue through one of these doors.

Enter

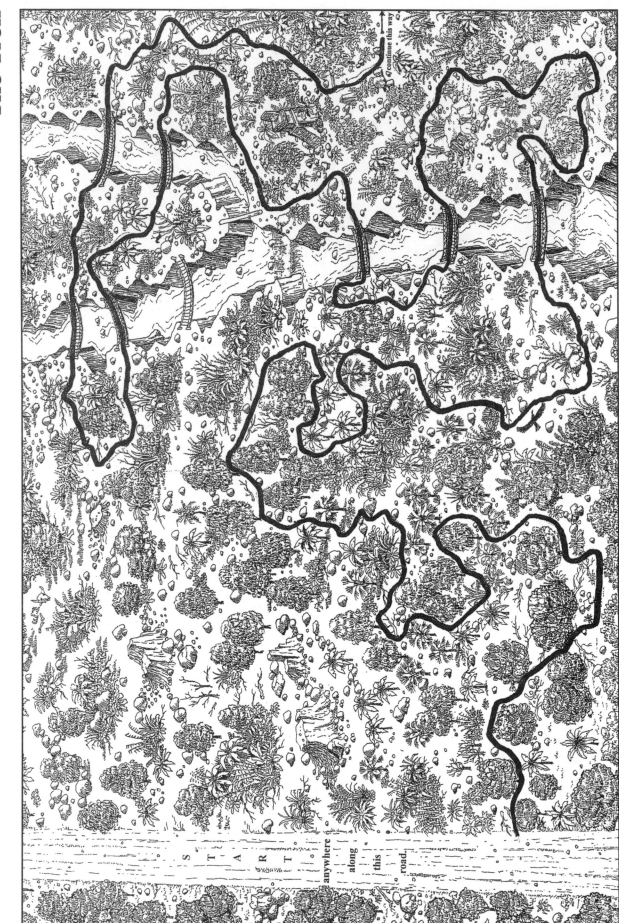

continue this way

START anywhere along this road.

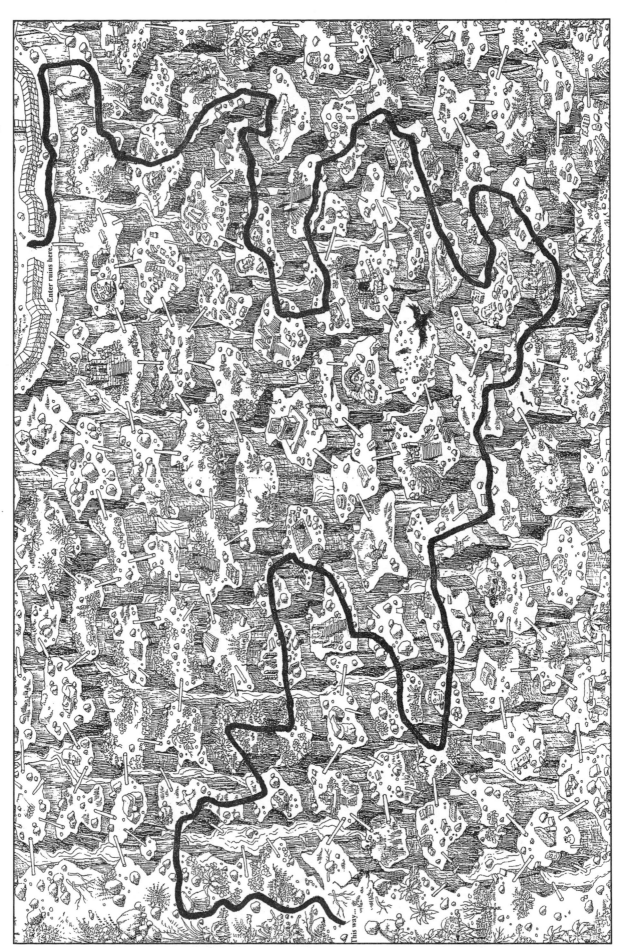

The Ruins

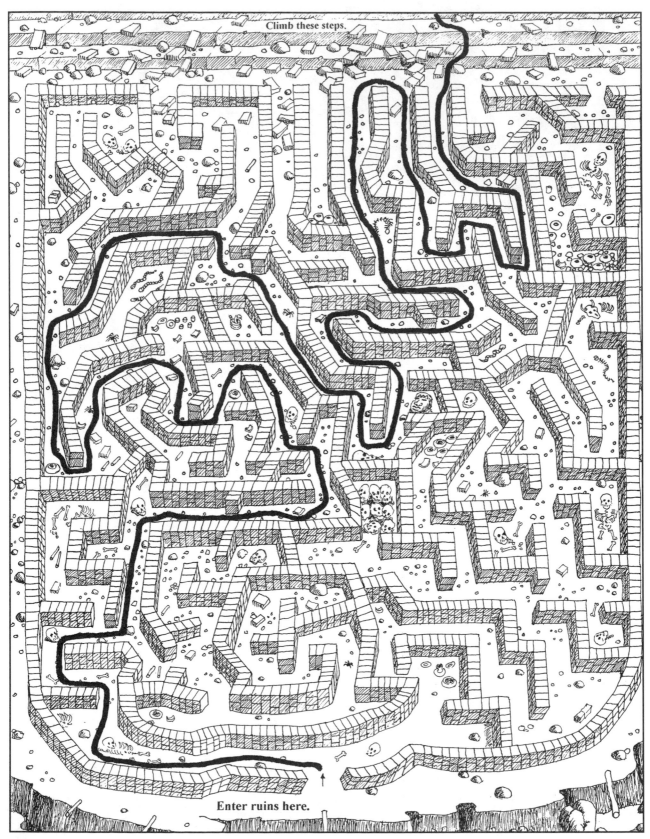

Climb these steps.

Enter ruins here.

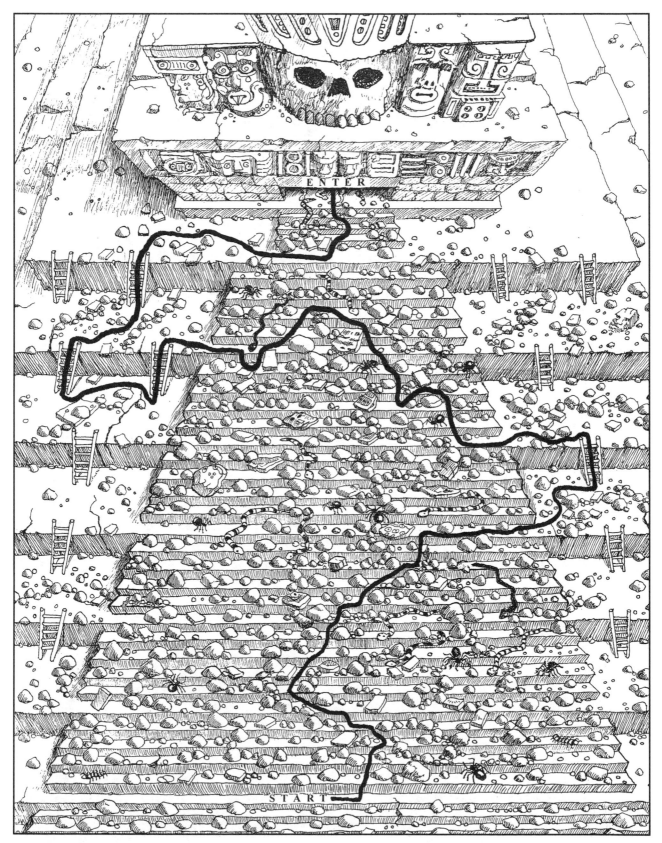

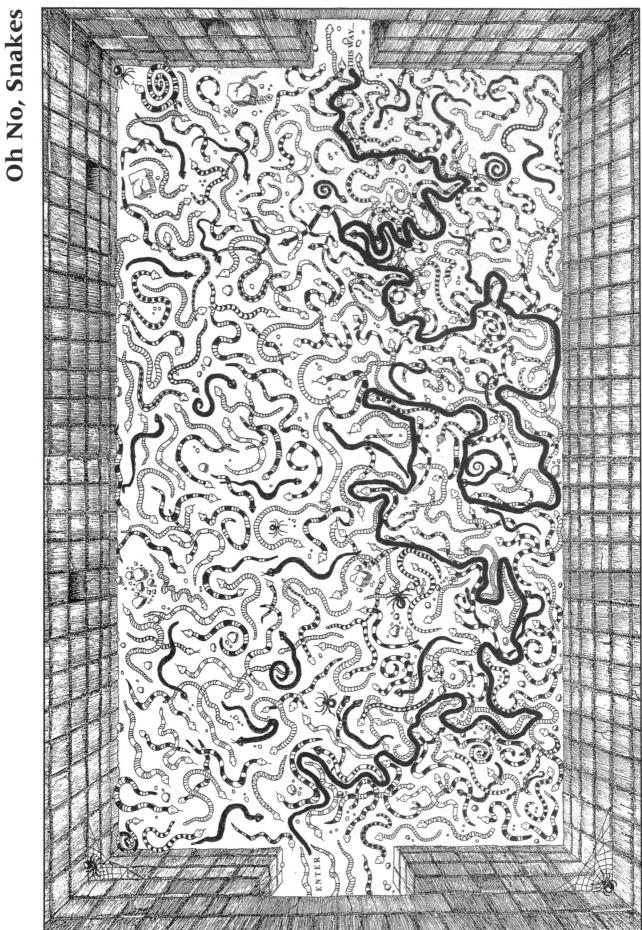

The Gold Idol

Exit through any of the 13 doors...if you can?

ENTER

63

Index

Treasure guides are noted in italics

Banquet Room, 28, *56*
Canyon Land, 34, *59*
Concepcion
   Map, 8, *44*
   Treasure, 10, *45*
Concepcion's Treasure, 10, *45*
Courtyard, 26, *55*
Cover maze, 4, *42*
Genoa's Buried Treasure, 5, 24, *53*
Gold Idol, 40, *63*
King John
   Banquet Room, 28, *56*
   Courtyard, 26, *55*
   Throne Room, 30, *57*
   Trail to the Castle, 25, *54*
King John's Throne Room, 30, *57*
Lost Dutchman Mine, 16, *49*
   Return to Phoenix, 18, *50*
Lost Mayan Temple, 37, *61*

Mayan temple
   Trek, 32, *58*
   Canyon Land, 34, *59*
   Ruins, 36, *60*
   Lost Mayan Temple, 37, *61*
   Oh No, Snakes, 38, *62*
   Gold Idol, 40, *63*
Money Pit 1, 14, *47*
Money Pit 2, 15, *48*
Oh No, Snakes, 38, *62*
Return to Phoenix, 18, *50*
Ruins, 36, *60*
S.S. *Central America*, 6, *43*
Sutro's Tunnel, 22, *52*
Trail to King John's Castle, 25, *54*
Treasure Map, 8, *44*
Treasure of Pinaki Atoll, 12, *46*
Trek, 32, *58*
Victorio Peak, 20, *51*